COOPERATING IN THE WORKPLACE

Revised and Expanded
Second Edition

by

Derrick Darden, PhD

Cooperating in the Workplace (Revised and Expanded Second Edition)

All rights Reserved.

Copyright © 2019 by Derrick Darden, PhD v2.0

PRINTED IN THE UNITED STATES OF AMERICA

Table of Contents

Dear Reader,

As our working environment becomes more diverse and global, our knowledge and organizational skills and behavior must develop along with those changes. Cooperating within the workplace is key and goes further than becoming competitive. In the words of Franklin D. Roosevelt, "Competition has been shown to be useful up to a certain point and no further, but cooperation, which is the thing we must strive for today, begins where competition leaves off."

As a Gulf War Veteran Army officer that worked in the fields of logistics and Federal Acquisition in the federal government and later as an entrepreneur, I've seen how organizational form and structure within the federal government and in my own business experience provided foundational keys and principles that has guided me to success in both the public and private sectors. Working together with co-workers, supervisors and management within organizations is the method for success. This book is a catalyst for situational understanding in navigating teams successfully and communicating to higher management. My experience in both perspective and practical will help the reader gain insight and those golden nuggets that can help get out of chaotic situations. If you are on a team or in leadership, developing the skills of Cooperation within the Workplace can prove successful for you and your organization.

Derrick Darden, PhD

Preface

The second edition is a total overhaul of the first book written on this topic of cooperating in the workplace. The author included practical steps and tips for the new employee, ways of taking charge of your work environment and much more. This expanded edition includes new trending topics that affect everyone in the workplace from the newly arrived employee to the CEO of the organization. These topics include working with Millennials and teamwork, dealing with sexual harassment in the workplace, the prevalence of drugs and alcohol in the workplace, working alongside veterans and working with teams. The author presents these topics from both governmental and private-sector perspectives in the United States and abroad. It is the author's intention to give the reader a wealth of information that can be used within the workplace and throughout life. Additionally, it is power-packed with past and current research bridging the gap between the both practical and theoretical in cooperating in the workplace.

Lastly, the second edition has the new employee solely in mind; however, a healthy workplace environment begins at the top of the organization, the leadership. Part two has hidden gems which I share from my experiences as a senior leader working both in the public and private workplace environments. This second edition helps the new employee navigate through the touch terrain and lay solid foundations that can help throughout a new career. Remember that "no man is an island, no man stands alone" (Author unknown). So, whether we are collaborating, communicating or agreeing with our co-workers, cooperating in the workplace should be the common goal of everyone within the organization.

Introduction

Business organizations are created for the purpose of making profits and returns on investment for their owners. In achieving maximum profit, there are various basic things that must be put in place by the owners and managers of a business organization. Apart from creating a formidable organizational structure, another important necessity is hiring effective employees for different sections or departments of the organization. It is important that the organization has effective policies and regulations that are targeted at ensuring that these employees work together for the success of the organization.

Cooperation is a process of working together toward the same end. It is a synergy of collaboration, and at its essence it takes compromise and a joint effort between involved parties to make an intended impact. Although there are many "keys" to making collaboration work in the workplace, the focus here is on communication, Decision making, Leadership and Teamwork.

There are always improvements that could be made to workplace cooperation, but the important first step is realizing cooperation in the workplace is necessary for success. We will help navigate the components of improving workplace cooperation, identify why communication skills are needed, discuss the importance of teamwork as well as cover common questions you may have.

Part One

(What is cooperating in the Workplace?)

Cooperating in the Workplace

Most of the activities of private and public organizations are founded on certain visions and missions and for these to be accomplished human beings are needed to carry out certain activities. There are various sections and departments that make an organization and each of them has defined roles and regulations towards achieving the common objectives of the organization. Therefore, there is need for interaction and cooperation between these people.

According to Gilani (2017), cooperation can be defined as working together for the purpose of achieving a common goal. This concept is needed in a workplace so that employees can work alongside each other to attain the objectives the management of the organization has set for them and those they have set for themselves. For employees to be productive they must work with each other.

Cooperating in the workplace has the ability to bring

success into a business and the lack of cooperation can lead to the failure of a business. When the management of an organization is able to create a framework or structure in which there is cooperation between the employees in the organization, they tend to communicate with each other effectively. This reduces argument or misunderstanding that could have arisen between the management and employees on the lower level in the organization (Schreiner, 2018). Cooperation among employees in a workplace can only be achieved through the creation of a healthy environment by the management of an organization such that each individual would be seen as important to the overall success of the organization and in such a way that every member of the organization would be made to understand that their individual contribution is just a part of the whole. Cooperation is built on the fact that each employee should be respected and valued by every other employee despite the variations in their beliefs and preferences (Darden, 2017).

However, because of the variations in the attitudes and behaviors of employees in a workplace it may not be easy to achieve cooperation and that is why it is important for the management of an organization to ensure that there are various regulations and policies in place to foster team work, communication and cooperation among their employees. This can be included in the organization structure of the business and it can be further strengthened through different seminars and workshops on cooperation in the workplace and the consequent effects on both the employees and the whole business organization (Lopes, Santos & Teles, 2009).

It is, nevertheless, important to point out that despite the fact that competition among employees in a workplace may be healthy to some extent, it cannot be compared to the positives and advantages that the cooperation among employees can bring to the organization.

Think of it this way - in this global enterprise, competitiveness is vital to the lifeblood of the organization. Ensuring that the life blood travels to the vital organs in order to remain functional, employees must carry it there by having the core skills necessary.

I recall in my anatomy and physiology class, we talked about the blood and how the blood is the life source that is vital to every organ in the body; without this the body will malfunction and die. The physiology of each organ needs to function as designed; the common thread is blood (red and white cells). These cells are vital to the inner workings of each organ (kidney, intestine, liver etc); if it doesn't have the nutrients and oxygen, the organs can malfunction and eventually become a burden to the body and eventually the overcompensation brings overload which results in a complete shut-down of the body. Could it have been avoided? In most cases yes, keep the flow of blood going consistently in order to avoid a malfunction within the body.

So, as the organization which is the organism (body) and which is built to function and withstand their competitive edge in that particular industry (auto, banking, IT), their survival depends on the lifeblood of their workforce. Without the lifeblood of the skilled employee the organization will malfunction. The employee brings the nutrients and oxygen to the vital organs (department, division or team) needed to survive. The core skills and abilities are those nutrients and oxygen to be brought to that single organ. Do you want your organization to stay alive and thrive? Then you as an employee must buy-in to its vision and mission. The attitude that everyone is expendable shouldn't permeate or be allowed in the organizational culture because every cell within the blood every nucleus that brings the vital nutrition to the organs of the body is needed, from the laborer to the manager is a part of each vital organ (organization). When you are a high performing employee within the organization you can find a direct correlation with high motivation, high productivity and high professionalism within your core being (Silver, 2000). You are motivated from within and not what someone can give you, reach within yourself. Researchers explains that motivation is an internal process that makes a person move toward a goal (Locke, Schattke, 2018).

Cooperation among employees has been defined as to be working together for the purpose of achieving a common goal. In a business environment, the common goal, vision and mission is mostly to bring profit to the owners of the business as well as to the workers in the organization.

Cooperating in a workplace is beneficial to the organization because it increases productivity as a result of the cohesion that exists between the employees. On the part of the employees, this can bring about job satisfaction. This happens as a result of the success that will be recorded because of the healthy environment created by cooperation. An employee will also benefit from the synergy that cooperation brings. Human beings have been identified by Aristotle to be social animals and, as a result of this, they have the natural tendency of relating with other people to bring about synergy.

Cooperating in the working place brings out the best in every employee since each individual will be helped by the other in achieving common goals of the organization. It is also beneficial to the organization by reducing misunderstandings and arguments that would have originally been felt in any working environment. This is possible because, cooperation brings about constructive criticism rather than destructive criticism and rather than competing, the employees will cooperate to achieve the goals of the organization. When there is cooperation in the workplace, employees that are involved have more tendency to engage in healthy competition among each other and also work in line with the vision and mission of the organization they are working for (Schreiner, 2018; Gilani, 2017).

How to Cooperate in the Workplace

As stated earlier, cooperating in a workplace is not easy because of the existence of competition among employees in many organizations. Disagreement among employees in a workplace is inevitable and it requires that an employee understands his or her role within the organization.

There are certain steps that can be followed in

achieving this and they are as stated below (Frost, 2018):

Identification of the goals, mission, and vision of the organization: each employee within the organization must be made to understand, by the management, the goals, visions and missions of the organization in which they are working. This should be instilled in them from their first day of work and must be consistently impressed upon them through different training and seminars. Vision is most important for an organization because it gives direction to its employees on the route the CEO wants to take and the goals he or she wants to obtain in a competitive environment. The employee of any organization must have a mission, goals and vision to live by. You (new employee) are the captain of your ship. You navigate the ship based on the course you wish to take.

Thinking back on my basic training days, I was with forty new recruits in Fort Knox, Kentucky. I had to spend over ten weeks with those recruits in close quarters; becoming highly proficient and efficient in physical fitness, weaponry, and psychological warfare. Basic training was a highly intense and challenging environment; after starting out with forty recruits, after ten weeks of training, thirty graduated the training program. Many dropped out for various reasons but making it to the level of being called a "soldier" was not as easy as it may sound. The Army defined my role, gave me a mission statement to believe in and a vision to follow. The organization must do the same, as far as having a mission that embraces the core values of the organization is concerned.

Define your role: in some cases, the management of the organization describes the roles and responsibilities of an employee in an organization, but, in a situation, where this is not defined, it is important for the employee to understand his or her role in achieving the goals and objectives of the organization both in the short term and long term. This will make the employee understand what is expected of him or her and also limit conflict of roles and responsibilities that may lead to arguments and misunderstandings in the workplace.

Attend meetings or work sessions: the employee must attend all the meetings in the organization that concerns him or her. This is necessary because most information needed to carry out his or her responsibilities will be discussed at these meetings and, so as to know the progress of the organization in achieving the goals that have been set, attendance is extremely important.

Relate well with others: cooperation can only be founded on a positive relationship. The employee must engage in efficient and effective relationship with other employees in the workplace. There should be open communication, sharing of ideas, healthy argument and criticism and courtesy among employees. The employee should also provide adequate feedback to the management on tasks and assignments giving and appropriate departments and sections in the organization must be consulted on areas that need their specialization.

A company can only be prosperous when the employees are cooperating towards achieving the goals of the organization. The management is tasked with the responsibility of creating healthy environments where cooperation amongst employees can be permitted thrive. To cooperate well in a workplace, employees must understand the goals, missions, and visions of the organization, know their responsibilities in achieving goals, be active in the programs and activities of the organization and, ultimately, they must relate well with each other and the higher levels of management.

Cooperating in the Workplace

Normally, when a person considers cooperation, especially in a workplace environment, they are simply thinking about ways to avoid chaos on the job or going with the flow, whether it's harmonious or chaotic. However, employees can be worlds apart in ideology and in their approach to various situations. For those trying to maintain a fulfilling workplace experience, there are certain steps that can be taken in order to realize that cooperating within the workplace can be as objective as possible and detrimental to one's career if unaware of the potential hidden landmines that lie among coworkers, supervisors, and upper management. As a new employee, knowing the environment or the culture of the organization demands your full attention. Cooperating demands action instead of passivity in which new employees will maintain the status quo.

After retiring from the military, I started my new career in the Federal Government as a civilian. I always envisioned reaching the top of that career no matter at what level I started from, as a journeyman or a team leader, so I started at the bottom and now I am a team leader and Contracting Officer responsible for millions of dollars in contract for the Federal Government. At every level there is a path to the next level and most employers want you to follow that path of progress in order to qualify for promotions or higher pay. Knowing what's going on in the organization is also important and sometimes it's a jungle trying to finding your career path in order to ultimately reach the top of your chosen profession.

I recall, prior to my military career, I got a job working for a utility company, which was a real step up, having come from a background and community that was deprived of opportunity. I started out as a meter reader, the bottom position within the company. However, every day, before I entered the doors of the high-rise building, I looked up at the very top office and envisioned having my own office up there, looking over the city, dressed in my suit and tie. How was I going to reach the top? By cooperating at the bottom and working within the systems that were laid out by this Fortune 500 company in relation to the career paths one can take to reach the top. Every day I was motivated by my vision which gave me the strength to, not only show up to work, but to go beyond what was required and expected of the meter readers. Every month I was amongst the top ten meter readers within the company because I took on the tough jobs that no one else wanted to do, but I also wanted to reach the top and, by knowing the terrain of the company and cooperating within my department, I became the number two meter reader within five months of starting the job. The unfortunate part of this story is that the culture of this company was toxic and jealous and afraid of emboldening newcomers from deprived backgrounds, so they let me go, and, just like that, I was unemployed. Again, I was not aware of the landmines hidden amongst my coworkers or supervisors.

Follow these three key steps which helped me:

Create your own atmosphere conducive for success

You probably already recognize that a successful atmosphere within the workplace can be created, although those who are unable or unwilling to work towards a harmonious approach to workplace cooperation may experience various challenges. The purpose of this book is to start you (new employee) on your journey towards making you aware and skillful in navigating the workplace environment. You determine your own destiny, so start charting your course.

Communicate with others to help reach a common goal

An integral part of establishing a foundation for effective cooperation in the workplace involves communicating while working towards a common goal. This is why good communication skills are pertinent between management and coworkers, as well as the entire work environment.

Communication, whether written or oral allows you to be in the right mindset to reach the basic goal of cooperating in the workplace.

Work together with your coworkers to complete projects

Working together with your coworkers to complete projects is an essential part of achieving proper workplace cooperation. If you are accustomed to utilizing teamwork and team building to complete projects, then working together becomes second nature. Working as a team is not a skill adoptable by all people, and it's important to recognize potential restrictions on the path towards improved teamwork.

We can examine certain preliminary practices that a person cooperating in the workplace should already be doing. Use this opportunity to incorporate these specific practices into your life, as they will ease the process of improving team communication.

Part of implementing improved workplace cooperation is recognizing employees who may already possess the skills you are hoping to achieve to attain your goal. These individuals will be links in the collaboration of your workplace.

There are numerous questions that you should ask yourself in order to outline goals in the workplace. The following questions are used to address specific goals:

- Do you like order and structure?
- Are you good at creating workable solutions to problems?
- Can you be a good team player?

Ideally, your reply to all three of these questions would be "yes."

Cooperating in the workplace takes a vast amount of effort invested over time. As a result, plans should be put in place that includes attainable timelines towards cooperative success. By having plans with timelines detailing your goals, you will be better able to prioritize from the outset. This is part of your preparation for cooperating in the workplace;

attaining this goal should include preparation aimed at the specific outcome you want to see obtained.

Time Wasters versus Time Management

As a new employee knowing what is effective versus what's not helps to get things done in a timely fashion. One thing I learned very quickly with the government is that meetings are a premium. We would joke about having meetings before the real meeting. I very soon got tired of these non-productive gatherings where, in quick succession, we would have had ten meetings and five of those would be non-productive.

For the manager, supervisor and individual worker, identification and elimination of time-wasting activities can foster an organization that promotes efficiency and increases productivity with increased profitability.

One time-waster that affects productivity is preoccupation with the wrong things instead of the task at hand. The good side of preoccupation is the focus that accompanies it, and I'm sure everyone has experienced this phenomenon. However, when it comes to our workers or our groups, we need to focus our attention on the individual task at hand. Now, some may argue that they can multi-task three or more things at once, but shifting the attention can actually be detrimental to both the individual and the culture. Focusing on two or more tasks impairs our judgment about what is worthy of our attention.

Poor communication in the workplace leads to performance problems and time-wasting activities. Preoccupation with the wrong things can lead to low quality and non-productive work.

Numerous meetings are unproductive with little end result. As reported in *Psychology Today*, a team of psychologists and neuroscientists have provided the explanation for why meetings are wasteful. It is agreed that we have a limited cognitive ability on a daily basis. This is diminished when we don't get enough sleep or take in the right amount of nutrients to help us focus, retain information and make decisions at these meetings. On the other hand, if meetings are necessary, we should always have an agenda. People should attempt to focus on the issues at hand, and must leave petty gossip and negative attitudes at the door. Meetings should take no more than one hour, and the less time the better. Finally, we need to create follow-up agendas for the next meeting, if we expect results to be attained with the intended benefits.

In order for time management to take the place of time-wasters, you need to have a plan. Although there are plenty of publications available about cooperating in the workplace, there is one common thing they all relay: the planning period is absolutely vital. The old saying is, "if you fail to plan, you plan to fail." This includes managing your time effectively and efficiently; we do this in life with retirement planning, marriage, and even starting a family. Cooperating within the workplace contributes to the overall goal of productivity and the avoidance of time-wasting. Sometimes, walking over to someone's cubicle and collaborating on priorities and tasks can avoid time-wasting meetings.

For the supervisor or manager, remember that you are responsible for the forward movement of the organization, in accordance with your mission plan, including operations, training of new personnel, and securing equipment and resources. You are the one who know where the weak links are within the organization. Managing your time and clearly laying out objectives will allow you to gain clarity while working towards your goal of improved cooperation. Through proper scheduling habits, organizational skills are maintained, while allowing for open communication and a better understanding of the task at hand. You should develop a plan for the next six to twelve months to tackle areas of deficiency within the organization. Don't wait until the busy season to start training folks, getting resources, and securing equipment. *Plan ahead to invest in the organization.* Workers should manage their time by establishing priorities. Schedule large projects up front and avoid disasters such as coworkers piling around your cubicle gossiping; reserve your workspace for productive work only. As a person who manages time well, reserve frivolous conversation for your breaks or lunchtime. Remember, the organization hired workers who are reliable, educated, and efficient. High efficiency increases productivity in the workplace, which then increases profitability for both the organization and the individual worker.

For the employee, know yourself and your fellow coworkers. If you know your own limitations, weaknesses and strengths, then you will be able to identify those things that are holding you back or, if you are a team lead, things that hold back your team from being the best they can be. Take care of yourself physically and mentally; don't be the that employee that stands in the way of your organization's progress; be a part of that progress. Don't be the problem, be the solution.

Lastly, there is no such thing as multi-tasking; research reveals that only a small percentage of the population has this skill. The rest of us are good at stopping one task and focusing on a new one, then going back to the first and picking up where we left off. However, statistics also show that multi-tasking lowers productivity and creativity, so the moral of the story is to focus on one thing at a time. If you do, then you will be successful at many things·

The golden nugget is this: avoid time wasters and be productive in the workplace. Employees, managers and supervisors need to examine their behaviors that may cause wasted time. Efficiency across the board is the name of the game. The new reality in the workplace is doing more with less. Organizations want cooperation from all their employees in order to produce a highly efficient, productive and satisfying work environment that fosters high output and produces a return on investment among all… this is what counts.

Rumor Control within the Workplace

As a new employee within the organization, don't perpetuate rumors. Employees affect the workplace environment in a negative way by spreading rumors that hurt or defame other coworkers. They are unsubstantial claims, inaccurate and mistaken beliefs. According to the author of *Rumors and Rumor control: A Manager's Guide to Understanding and Combating Rumors,* rumors usually appear through situations of extreme stress, mistrust and confusion. Further, they can also thrive on these irrelevant facts or die a slow death when the crisis has subsided.

Example 2:
You're working in a facility in a small town where everyone knows your name. Then, one day, someone sees you riding in a car with what appears to be a young single woman, not once but twice. Two people have spotted both of you together and they tell their friends that a relationship is happening between you. Now these friends tell others and so on. Two weeks later this information gets back to

you. You know that nothing has happened, and the woman who was with you, who is in fact married, is innocent in all of this. You wonder how you can stop the embarrassment and shame that has tarnished your names.

Rumors can cause high anxieties. However, rumors can help promote positive information as well. Rumors or gossip are particularly useful within the organization. You may ask how? It's through the grapevine method. Some researchers estimate that, through this method, seventy-five to ninety percent of information disseminated is factual.. A company grapevine can show whether an organization is healthy or not. Rumors can hurt an individual or a group of people, but rumors can also promote positive ideas to others in your organization too.

In a landmark study conducted by researchers Allport and Postman (1947), it was concluded that, as rumors travel from person to person, they become shorter and easier to comprehend. Furthermore, seventy percent of the details in the message is lost during repetitive transmission of the rumor.

While quite obviously laden with negative connotations, what, if any, intrinsic values do rumors present? Researcher Kimmel (2004) evaluated that rumors present the basics of how humans interact with each other. So whether these rumors are negative or positive they have the capacity to address our human desires, needs and wants. Organizations can benefit through the spreading of rumors and gossip in the workplace. Researchers found that rumors or gossip in organizations can sustain and perpetuate positive factors within the organization. These positive factors perpetuate clarity and understanding of the social structure within the organization. They also point out important ramifications for relationships and formal structure within the workplace. Finally, rumors or gossip can protect the organization by offering individuals informal social mobility, influence and escapism.

Another positive influence that organizations can have on the flow of communication within the workplace is to use the grapevine to control what information is transmitted. According to Dr. Robbins (2004), author of *Essentials of Organizational Behavior*, the grapevine experience can be beneficial to managers by knowing the morale levels within the organization. Next, this same experience can help the manager understand the uncertainties and stresses amongst their employees. Lastly, the manager can understand and evaluate how formal and informal communication effectively is assimilated within the organization.

If you want to stop the rumors or gossip from spreading, there are a number of methodologies, both credible and non-credible. It depends on your situation and how effectively you want the results to manifest. Rumors or gossip can be mentally stressful to an individual or a group.

Psychological Impacts of a Negative Workplace

Employees can disrupt the work environment by harassing and upsetting coworkers. As a new employee become aware of your workplace environment positive or negative and if it's conducive to your overall health physically and mentally. Working in a negative workplace has psychological impacts, studies have shown. Researchers have found a growing national trend in employees experiencing some form of negative behavior in the work environment. A study conducted by two researchers Bowling and Beehr (2006) is credited for introducing a theoretical model that associates negative behaviors in the workplace and its possible origins and significances from the victims point of view. Furthermore, the 2006 study of U.S. workers found that over forty-one percent or approximately 47 million American workers reported being involved at their workplace with psychological antagonism over the past twelve months (Bowling,T.A. & Beehr (2006). In a survey conducted by the U.S. government in 2012, it was found that 1 in 8 witnessed some kind of form of negative behavior in the workplace (Federal Government, 2012). Studies into negative workplace behaviors and their environments have researchers looking at the causal relationship between work-related psychosocial hazards and psychological illness. Some negative behaviors that can be seen in an individual or a group are manipulation and exploitation, bullying, degradation, humiliation and harassment; this was shown in a 2006 study which indicates a relationship between various behaviors such as depression, anxiety and physical symptoms.

Researchers found that negative behavior in the workplace and an employee's intention to leave the organization has an indirect link to ill-health.

These studies confirm that when employees experience the negative effects of psychological workplace hazards and the above-mentioned behaviors are displayed amongst the individual or group, it results in high absenteeism and huge turnover rates in the organization. The European study proves this link between high turnovers and exposed to negative workplace environments. The Study was conducted at the University of Copenhagen Psychology Department:

In this study, 2,154 healthcare workers were followed for three years to investigate the risk of turnover when exposed to a negative environment at the workplace. In the first year, the study found that 9.2% of the workers responded to a negative environment on a frequent basis. In years two and three, they saw a strong correlation between frequent exposure to a negative work environment and high turnover rates. This study also pointed out the correlation between the health of the worker and work conditions. Three factors stood out in this study regarding why these workers wanted to quit: poor leadership, constant exposure to negative behavior and health problems, which can affect the worker in the long term. As a result, organizations experience high absenteeism and high turnover that ultimately ends with low productivity, poor creativity and a decline in work quality (Hogh, Hoel, & Caneiro,2011).

All of this hampers an organization's ability to compete in a competitive environment, to hire and retain talented individuals, and to foster a healthy work environment. Negative behaviors should not be tolerated in the workplace. It is too costly for the organization and the individual. Additionally, it undermines the goals, vision and, ultimately, the success of the organization. Cooperating within the workplace as an employee embraces the organization's policies and regulations regarding producing a positive work environment. Take action whenever this negative behavior is exposed in an organization, a zero-tolerance policy should be implemented throughout the organization. If you are a managers and leaders monitor the work environment on a constant basis. Remember, a negative workplace environment affects all employees; cooperating to produce a positive workplace environment affects us all, also.

Communication is Key

Communication, within the workplace, or on the battlefield determines predictability or a positive outcome to a co-worker, soldier or a team member. Authors Robbins and Finley (2000) describe communication as the heart of the team in the exchange of information and the delegation of work. The bottom line is that without the correct communication flowing throughout, the team can greatly inhibit their own performance level. The key points of communication are the sender, the receiver and the message.

The sender communicates the message; the audience receives the message then interprets it. The message makes an impact on the audience. Hopefully the interpretation is right, if not, then misunderstood messages can cause conflict. Distorted messages are usually a product of bias towards it. Trust can also hamper the good intentions of the sender. In the military, clear and concise communication is essential for any military unit. Distorted miscommunication can cause fatalities on the battlefield. Effective communication for a team is not an easy thing. Because of the distortions that can cloud effective communication, the team must work hard in recognizing barriers and promote better interpersonal skills.

Listening skills are central to the team's ability to provide feedback through paraphrasing ideals and phrases. Listening, especially active listening, promotes feedback to the initiator of the message.

The moment you make the decision to seek improved workplace cooperation, it's imperative that strategies be laid out in order to ensure productivity and efficiency.

Working as a team within the workplace requires a high level of dedication, at which point skills already discussed — such as organization and planning — will aid towards success. Teamwork is also essential to project completion.

It is important to voice your intention of improved communication amongst staff members, as well as improving overall cooperation as it encourages others to get in a similar mindset. The section about organization is key to this, as well, and is one of the key secrets of developing a cooperative and functional workplace environment. Others need to be able to see that they are stepping into an environment free of chaos, which will allow them to alter their focus in order to line up with various new strategies.

Communicating with others to help reach a common goal is also essential when it relates to planning towards consciously improved teamwork, which is part of the reason that you want to state your intentions. This will help in creating an atmosphere conducive for success, leading to improved productivity. It may seem like a minute or effortless step, but it cements your intentions. This will also reduce the amount of stress amongst coworkers, as a common goal is being put in place. All employees need to recognize the positive outcomes that could potentially arise from increased cooperation.

Communication: The Tool of Loyalty

Two things I long to see strengthened in my federal government organization are better communication and a more earnest display of loyalty. In the military, loyalty reflects the army values which are instilled within every soldier who takes the Oath of Allegiance. A solder is loyal and will defend this country's constitution and this country's interest at home or abroad. Cooperating within the organization's mission and vision statement displays a loyal behavior that should be seen from the top down throughout the whole organization. Policies and regulations are adhered to without deviations unless instructed to do so. Researchers explain that "effective leadership occurs when the communication of leaders and subordinates is characterized by mutual trust, respect and commitment." Much information doesn't make its way down the chain to the subordinate levels. Often, valuable information is held by someone intentionally. Some find themselves explaining to their supervisors why they didn't get that report out or why they missed the meeting. To resolve this communication problem in my organization, I would suggest developing a feedback system that ensures that your messages were received by the intended party. The top managers should have regular counseling sessions with departments within their area of responsibility. Secondly, when sending out important email messages, select the option that prompts the receiver to acknowledge and reply back to you. Furthermore, CEO's should have corporate meetings with all employees within the organization; this is a good way of communicating updated information and gauging the culture climate.

Loyalty, in the military, is bearing true faith and allegiance to the U.S. constitution, the Army, your unit, and your comrades. This is extended to your country and your mission. In the private sector, employees put their trust in the company they work for. Being a good and faithful employee means believing in the company's mission and striving to help the company benefit from your efforts. It's important to be respectful and friendly to fellow employees regardless of stature. I feel this is an atmosphere for loyalty to develop in the organization. It's up to the leadership to foster and nurture this trait or behavior in all levels of the organization.

Cooperating in Everyday Life

Even though workplace cooperation may not occur every day, the skills involved in the creation of cooperative tasks or cooperation, which are executed in everyday life are essential as you consistently make improvements, which will, likewise, be felt in everyday habits.

The earlier questions you asked yourself are not just inherent personal characteristics, but are capable of giving you results in any situations in life.

Cooperating within the workplace is not easy while climbing the corporate ladder but it's worth the effort. There is more to cooperating in the workplace than mere thought; establishing the required skills for the accomplishment of this goal will inevitably reach out to everyday life, including enhancing organizational skills. My saying is *"Everything nice comes with a price,"* what are you willing to sacrifice? Be conscious of the fact that the dedication and efforts in the establishment of this goal will not be in vain. The Army has a few slogans that helped me through many rough journeys through life "be all that you can be" and "*Army Strong*". Recognize that the required work for these goals are important for the increasing core skills and abilities, being situationally aware of trendy topics such as working with Millennials, dealing with sexual harassment in the workplace, working alongside veterans and working with teams. This second edition is a power pack in making you an asset within your work environment.

The bottom line upfront is, those that are the most dedicated will experience the success of their goals. You can be part of this group. If you permit your mind to become cooperative within your workplace environment, you will realize how exciting this journey is – **I wish you all the best as you take this step!**

Something to focus on about cooperating in the workplace

It is easier to achieve the goals of improved workplace cooperation when you know everyone has the same ambitions. However, as much as this is a general goal, the reality is that just only a small number of people will move forward, act, and be capable of realizing their goals so as to achieve them. That being said, it is essential that at the initial stage, your specific goals should be such that you are capable of accounting for them. You determine your own destiny. You launched your capability of setting goals and adhering to them when answering some questions like:

- **"How much do you like structure and order?"** This relies on the employee to realize how flexible he or she is within a structural environment,

- **How focused you are when working on projects with co-workers**? It is time you measured your readiness to commit effort and time to ensure your workplace collaboration with your coworker, supervisor and management are successful.

You will discover that there is a common attribute among employees who exhibit proper workplace cooperation: they are fully aware of what they are doing. They all value the potential results of improved workplace cooperation, just as they understand the required communicative skills in their workplace, and that of their team members. Thus, successful team players know what is involved to achieve a particular goal. Your positive response to the question of **"can you be a good**

team player?" ascertains how ready you are to work with others, with a level of competency and discipline. At this time, you can start building the required resources to enable you, and to facilitate your team, to achieve a more suitable cooperative environment with the organization.

Tangible outcomes accompany proper workplace cooperation; for instance, the possibility of coming up with positive outcomes will be increased with advance preparation. Therefore, organizational skills are necessary as the individual will, likewise, have to remain resourceful so as to work cooperatively with other people. Your resourcefulness was ascertained when you answered questions of how valuable you are through taking on the easy jobs, now "are you good at creating workable solutions to problems?"

Clearly, answering the above questions truthfully, enable you to determine if you have all the required attributes to work efficiently in a cooperative work environment. Being honest is extremely important when providing answers to these questions as some people who were unable to accomplish workplace cooperation did so due to unreadiness to undertake the required task. When you ask yourself about these particular goals, you make a contribution towards a positive outcome.

It is essential to consider the goals you intend to achieve in your workplace, particularly in respect of cooperation. The best way to do this is by considering the importance of cooperation in daily life. Starting when you open your eyes in the morning and closing them at night. In what ways do you cooperate in your everyday life? Connecting these dots will make it simpler to direct your workplace to improved cooperation. Remember, "you can determine your own destiny".

Part Two

(Treading topics that affect every workplace environment)

Working with Millennials and Teamwork

Millennials in the workplace are heavily stereotyped, with widespread media portraying them as unmotivated, self-centered, disrespectful, and anti-authoritarian. These are not true claims. Millennials embrace teamwork and group dynamics in the workplace. They will be the change Agent we, as leaders, will only imagine.

Communication, motivation and decision making are vital when it comes to making it work in the workplace (Kozlowski,& Ligen, 2006). These are traits that many assume Millennials lack. However, the empirical evidence surrounding this does not seem to conclude that such is the case. While Millennials do seem to want ideals and a workplace culture that is different than previous generations have, the idea that they are bad workers seems to be more because Millennials have different mindsets—and, as a result, different values, than previous generations.

Studies show that teamwork is the preferred method of Millennials (Hannam, Yordi,B. (2011). This is important because this can have both beneficial applications, as well as harmful effects on many aspects of employment. For example, while Millennials may prefer to use group consensus as a way to impact decision-making, some decisions, regardless of position in the company, have to be made at a moment's notice. Why? Because teams can take time to form, and that time may be something that is not always available. Using group consensus can become an issue to group dynamics since teams tend to develop their own control systems. This can cause members to conform to norms within the group, and make them unlikely to question issues when they see them (Greer,2014). We the Baby Boomer generation knows all too well this scenario and it is in every business book that addresses group dynamics. "Group Think" under President Kennedy his group of advisors "go with the flow" mentality almost caused a major collusion with Russia in the fiasco called the "Bay of Pigs".

Managers and Supervisors need to recognize the signs and avoid group thinking; a few suggest a reduction in team size to no more than ten members. Secondly, invite different perspectives into the decision-making process. Thirdly, chose a person who is contradictory. A team needs a person that will challenge the status quo - a devil's advocate. Fourthly, seek outside opinions in order to help the organization to form and shape the decision. This is covered in the team section of this book.

Getting back to why do Millennials like to work in teams so often? This is an easy question to answer if you look at the evidence. The reason why Millennials like working in groups is because it lowers the workload, increases the chances for success, provides social relationships and increases job satisfaction as opposed to working by themselves. Since Millennials are highly social, due to the advent of social media platforms like Facebook, working in groups helps them to feel more a part of the company, as opposed to just a worker.

Popular media refers to Millennials as the "me me me" generation, claiming that they are lazy, entitled and narcissistic. Is this a fair comparison of them as a group, or is this more about the bias of older generations? The evidence seems to suggest the latter, as Millennials seem to have differing views on how to approach the same problems as older generations might approach them. For instance, the latter may see the former's desire for knowledge about otherwise "need to know" information, even as a newcomer, as disrespectful. It should be noted that Millennials do not see it as such.

The mindset of the Millennial, such as needing constant feedback and enjoying collaboration, seems to work well when it comes to group dynamics. Because of this, Millennials are more likely to be active in their involvement and try their best when the work is done as a team, as opposed to individually. The increase in technology has also helped Millennials form groups even outside of the workplace, which has caused a whole new dynamic to be created as opposed to older generations as well.

Millennials expect close relationships, even with managers, and expect frequent feedback whenever possible. This can become grating for many older generations who prefer to work individually and are used to self-grading on how well they did. However, within their own group, they seem to thrive the best. They are likely to self-manage their own teams and are even likely to form internal power structures and increase communications as opposed to older generations (Myers & Sadaghiani 2010)

Bottom line up front: the ability to work in a group and understand group dynamics is vital to any workplace. This is confounded by numerous differences between Millennials and other generations, such as Baby Boomers and Generation X. The diversity of Millennials in terms of race, sex, gender, culture, and even religious beliefs makes them hard to pinpoint as individuals, yet still able to be understood as a group. The different mindsets between Millennials and other generations make it hard for them to see eye to eye on many levels but make it easy for Millennials to work together among themselves on a team or in a cohesive group. Also, while it may seem to older people that Millennials are just lazy and dislike authority, the evidence shows that Millennials enjoy working, have a preference of teamwork and most often to see eye to eye with their supervisors. A mind shift towards this generation of workers is taking place and will soon become our next leaders in politics and in industry.

Sexual Harassment and Abuse in the Workplace and on College Campuses

We all have been bombarded with the news and social media on the latest victims and perpetrators of sexual harassment and abuse cases from Hollywood, the corporate office and the common person within the workplace together with the ill treatment of women and men as far as entertaining unwanted sexual advances. I believe that our society, as we know it, is not accepting this type of behavior any longer, this is why convictions are being felt from high profile cases from Harvey Weinstein, Bill Cosby and many others.

Sexual harassment and abuse in the workplace can be defined as unwanted sexual relations imposed on subordinates by superiors at work. Sexual harassment or its components 'were not contained in the original Sex Discrimination Act of 1975. The definition on the amended act in 2005 defined it as *'unwanted discrimination on the basis of their sex.* Both sexes are harassed but women are most likely to be the victims (Ramsaroop & Parumasur, 2007).

The victims of sexual harassment are usually younger and hold lower positions in the workplace (Hersch, 2015). The term "sexual harassment" was coined by feminists in the United States in 1975 to describe male's sexual coercion and exploitation of females in the workplace.

Sexual harassment occurs in almost all industries and occupations and the culture of these organizations is the key to understanding how it occurs in various places. Sexual harassment is more prevalent in occupations with unequal sex ratio, during periods of job insecurity, where there exists large power differentiation between males and females and when new managers are appointed (Merkin, 2012).

The practice of sexual harassment began centuries ago, especially in the chattel slavery endured by females of color without protection by law (Siegel, 2003). Crucial differences existed in situations where free women worked in domestic services, although they also faced sexual harassment by males in the households in which they were employed. Men assaulted women working for them especially in the clerical and manufacturing positions in the late nineteenth and early twentieth centuries. Most females lived within constraints that limited their expectations and aspirations of waged work, and they treated the workplace as a temporary way station and located their identities and economic destinies in the homes. Women who chose to work, including those of color who remained in the labor force, were highly discriminated against. Women who rebelled and transgressed the limits, fended off the physical and verbal assault with humor and had to endure the harassing behavior or turn away in silence.

The Civil Rights Movement Act of 1964 began to change the issue of workplace harassment (Baker, 2007). The Act forbade discriminatory behaviors on the grounds of race, sex and religion. Despite having the Act in place, men still derived greater benefits from the workplace than their female counterparts. The notion was challenged by court cases especially in 1972 where an African-American employee in the Justice Department of the United States, Diane Williams, sued to get her job back after she was dismissed for refusing to sleep with her boss. More cases followed and sexual harassment became prohibited legally by the early 1980s on the grounds that it restricted women's options and limited their opportunities in the workplace. Although some women sued for jobs and damages successfully, the people's culture was not changed by legal decisions. Sexual coercion still remained endemic in the workplace, deeply reinforced by normative assumptions about female's nature and deeply rooted in the gendered relationships.

The causes of occupational sexual harassment and abuse are a manifestation of power relations (Juliano, 2007). The hostility of males towards females is closely associated with males' attitudes about their role in society. Data about the United States indicates that ten percent of women have been assaulted sexually or raped in their lifetime while more than fifty percent of women living with their husbands have experienced some kind of domestic violence like battering. Sexual harassment is also contributed to by the women's economics at work. The entry of most women in the labor-force is driven by necessity to make ends meet for single-parent families or those with wife and husband not working full-time. This contributes to the exploitation of the presence of females as they submit to sexual behaviors to retain their work and positions. Discrimination is used to control workers by forcing women into poorly-paying jobs and using sexual harassment to keep them there (McLaughlin, Uggen & Blackstone, 2012). Tolerance of sexual harassment is a crucial enabling factor for the harassers especially in group environments such as the military where behaviors of harassment are curtailed without a supportive infrastructure

(Gerdes, 1999). The hierarchical structure in the United States military increases the risks of sexual harassment based on abuse of authority because leaders can change policies dramatically to favor their needs (Stander & Thomsen, 2016).

Social Progress in Handling Sexual Harassment and Abuse

Some blinders on sexual harassment and abuse in the workplace were removed by societal changes. Women's movements in the 1960s called for attention to the mysticism surrounding females' home roles. The movements were followed by a dramatic rise in the number of females searching for jobs. Almost half of the workforce was made up of women by the early 1990s and they wanted to share the rewards of good jobs. Women demanded equal or comparable pay, for an end to glass ceilings and discriminatory seniority rules, and raised hackles of males unaccustomed to the competition of that kind (McLaughlin, Uggen & Blackstone, 2012). The family became a fixture and men softened their resistance to women's wages because they were no longer expected to support families (Baker, 2007). Women became the primary wage earners in the early twentieth century. They were now able to protest the inequalities and daily humiliations more loudly because they had been released from the restrictions of the home.

A wide range of organizations has published guides on good practice. The guides cover relevant issues from sexual harassment and abuse prevention to follow-ups. The organizations have well-established procedures and policies, workforce training and senior staff support and commitment. Most organizations have also changed the organizational culture to not tolerate harassment, and implement appropriate monitoring systems and provide victims with independent support (Hunt, Davidson, Fielden & Hoel, 2007). As a new employee or manager it is your job to know the policies and guidelines on this topic and the proper protocol on how to report problems or issues that may come up when they happen. The Human Resource Department should have this outlined in the employee handbook.

Prevention of Sexual Harassment and Abuse

The potential solutions for preventing occupational sexual harassment and abuse include training. The training sheds light on the types of behaviors that constitute sexual harassment (Roehling & Huang, 2018). Thorough training provides the individual with insight on sexual harassment and on what is legal as well as their personal   rights.

Sexual harassment and abuse in the workplace can be prevented by educating students. The lessons should be included in the education system because instances of sexual harassment have escalated across colleges. Mandatory training and education will enable members of the community to stand up to violators and eradicate sexual harassment.

Sexual assault in the workplace can be prevented by holding people accountable for their actions. The harassers, as well as those who let sexual harassment happen, should be held accountable for their actions. Victims of sexual harassment should be supported by their peers and supervisors.

More effective policies should be applied to fighting sexual violence and abuse. The laws, requirements, and punishments should be made stricter (Joubert, Van Wyk & Rothmann, 2011). The perpetrators of sexual violence should not be allowed to get away with it because they are a problem to their peers. As far as resolving sexual harassment and abuse in our educational institutions, Secretary DeVos pasted sweeping changes regarding new procedures in higher learning institutions and handling sexual harassment on campus.

The Prevalence of Drugs and Alcohol Contributes to Violence in the Workplace

Addiction is an epidemic in the United States. The National Institute on Drug Abuse estimates that approximately sixty-eight percent of illegal drug users are employed full or part-time. One out of every ten people in the United States has an alcohol problem. There's a very good chance that someone where you work abuses alcohol or other drugs. A new employee or manager should be aware of the growing epidemic of over-use of opioids in the workplace environment. America has a serious drug problem. The effects of the opioid epidemic are severe when it comes to public health and social and economic stability in the workplace environment in the United States. The following impact is experienced among the workers in their workplace. Record from the Center for Disease Control indicates that approximately two hundred Americans die daily from opioid overdoses. The illicit opioid is heroin whereas the synthetic includes Fentanyl among numerous pain prescriptions.

Users of opioids experience some side effects such as alteration of their mental state, slowed breathing, constipation, nausea and drowsiness. When overdosed, the person may develop unresponsive respiratory problems and depression, which leads to other related cases (Volkow & McLellan, 2016). As a result, many workers are rendered unproductive because they tend to expend their energies fighting the effect rather than concentrating on their work-related responsibilities.

Besides the loss in productivity and healthcare expenses, employers must pay for the cost of treating an employee with an opioid epidemic addiction (Califf, Woodcock & Ostroff, 2016). Also, there are legal concerns employers must regard - preserving privacy and protecting medical information of the employee, mainly if an employee tests positive for opioids that may not be an addiction problem but a dependency on the drug.

The problem is that employers wanting to maintain a drug-free workplace environment, have to consider such elements as drug testing to establish whether the job task is done in a risk-free environment and safer manner (Volkow & McLellan, 2016), all whilst protecting the privacy of the employee and staying within the legal arena without exposing wrong information about the employee.

However, these are challenging times for employers, not only in maintaining productive employees, but keeping a safe work environment and protecting those employees that are taking legitimately prescribed medication.

The departments of Health and Human Services and the National Institute of Health are working with pharmaceutical companies and educational research institutions to come up with ways to ease or end the addiction problem in America.

Employees with substance abuse problems are far less productive, miss more days of work and are more likely to injure themselves or someone else and file more workers' compensation claims. The employer cannot absorb all of the costs, and therefore must pass the cost on to all employees in the form of higher insurance premiums and reduced salaries and benefit packages. There are hidden costs too: stress to others who fill in for the absent workers, damage to equipment, a drain on supervisory time, and reduction in high quality patient care.

At any given time, roughly ten percent of the United States populace is mishandling medications and liquor, with large numbers of families, companions, neighbors, managers, and colleagues being specifically influenced. The expenses related to medication and liquor add up to about $600 billion in lost income, medicinal services, lawful charges, and harms every year. Medications misuse is related to higher rates of increase sexual assault in schools, increase jail sentences and lost profitability, combined with expanded business related wounds. The individuals who misuse medication and alcohol will probably take part in hazard-taking practices, have a higher co-event of mental issues and will probably be imprisoned for wrongdoings much more frequently than those who do not indulge in such practices.

All in all, substance abuse can have a profound impact on both the productivity and safety of a workplace. If your company doesn't already have an alcohol and drug abuse policy and testing program in place, take a moment to consider the effects of substance abuse in the workplace.

All psychoactive substances have, to a higher or lesser extent, a dysfunctional effect on work capability (Kauert & Breitstadt 2008; Schuckjt, 2009). A worker under the effect of a psychoactive substance becomes a hazard to him/herself and to others around. Even if the deviant behavior is not readily visible or detectable, this person has a reduced ability to identify and control hazards – this incapacity suggests the need to address alcohol and drug abuse in the workplace (Baer and Hess, 2008).

The abuse of psychoactive substances is associated with many adverse consequences to health (Chipman & Jun, 2009; Degenhardt and Hall, 2012; Schuckjt, 2009) and consequently to safety at work, such as violence, accidents (Li and Bai, 2008), injuries (Trent, 1991) and absenteeism.

Workplace violence can be generally defined as verbal and physical assault or any violence that occurs in the workplace even if its source is unrelated to the work environment; self-directed assault, such as suicide, is included. Violence in the workplace takes many forms, from raised voices and profanity or sexual harassment, to larceny, robbery or assault and battery. The numbers of physical assault and battery are rising, and in spite of media hype, the attacker is not usually a disgruntled employee. Employee use of drugs and alcohol can result in reduced effectiveness at work and an increase in violence. Workers who abuse drugs and alcohol at the worksite increase the risk of engaging in intimidation or violence with coworkers.

Every business owner focuses on the bottom line,

so let's start with the costs of substance abuse. Substance abusers cost employers an average of $13,000 a year (Kauert & Breitstadt, 2008). In total, this costs the American economy $81 billion annually, as approximately seventy percent of the 14.8 million Americans who abuse illegal drugs are employed (Kauert, 2008). This loss of revenue results from decreased productivity (which we will discuss in more detail below) as well as workers' compensation claims, health care costs, legal liabilities, and theft. Employees who abuse drugs or alcohol are three to five times more likely to file workers' compensation claims. Plus, employee substance abuse can increase your healthcare costs by 300%! (Kauert, 2008).

It should come as no surprise, then, that substance abuse reduces productivity in the workplace. After all, drug and alcohol use often causes poor concentration, a lack of focus, carelessness and errors in judgment (Trent, 1991). Substance abuse can lower your business's productivity by one-third and cause two and a half times more absenteeism. Plus, workers who abuse alcohol are 2.7 times more likely than other workers to have injury-related absences (Trent, 1991).

Employees who abuse alcohol or drugs during or before work are more likely to sleep on the job, lack attention, and struggle to concentrate (Trent, 1991). They may be preoccupied with obtaining and using substances while at work, and they are also more likely to suffer lost-time injuries (i.e., an injury or accident that leads to the loss of productive work time).

Additionally, employees who abuse drugs or alcohol tend to hop between jobs. This high turnover rate is bad news for employers, who will waste time interviewing, hiring and training new employees.

Drugs and alcohol can dramatically change a person's behavior, and these negative changes in personality may lower your workplace morale. For example, the abuser may be tardy, lethargic, defensive, or quick-tempered. They may suffer from stress due to financial problems, complain about issues at home, or blame their coworkers for their own mistakes and shortcomings. Sometimes abusers will neglect their personal hygiene and appearance and they may exhibit symptoms of a hangover or withdrawal.

Just as one bad apple can spoil the whole bunch, one employee can alter the morale of the entire workplace. Coworkers may resent the substance abuser's lack of productivity, especially if this person is often late or absent, resulting in the coworkers suffering stress and frustration as they try to cover the neglected duties.

Due to impaired judgment, a lack of concentration and a variety of other side effects, substance abusers are more likely to cause injuries, accidents, and even fatalities in the workplace. In fact, one-fifth of workers and managers have reported that a coworker's on-the-job or off-the-job drinking hurt their productivity and/or jeopardized their safety. Substance abuse is the third leading cause of workplace violence, and drug-using employees are 3.6 times more likely to be involved in workplace accidents, especially in industries that involve dangerous equipment, locations, or duties - substance abuse can be deadly (Irvine, 1995).

Drug Testing Offers a Solution

The effects of substance abuse in the workplace can be frustrating, upsetting, and devastating. Luckily, you can greatly reduce the prevalence of this by creating a firm drug-free (and alcohol free) policy, educating your employees and implementing a testing program. Not only would this benefit your company's bottom line, but it would also improve the lives of your employees.

Working Alongside Veterans

Veterans are now ranked as a top recruiting target for companies, underscoring the commitment to, and investment in, veterans being made by American businesses but the problem according to researchers Abrams & Kennedy (2015), senior fellows at the research think tank Center for Talent Innovation track record, particularly among veterans in professional careers, is not very well understood. A survey conducted by both researchers with 1042 veterans working full-time concluded that companies spend twenty to thirty percent of their recruiting budget on hiring veterans but they are unable to make use out of that money, the reason being either veterans are not willing to rise or they are eager to advance but have trouble getting promoted. Many veterans feel under-utilized, alienated and uninspired in corporate workplaces. Fully two-thirds of the respondents said they were not using three or more of the skills they have that could be applicable to their employers.

False assumptions of coworkers such as 'veterans

are politically conservative due to their military background' are another issue that is very common. Veterans avoid sharing their military experiences with their colleagues, For fear of being stigmatized for having a mental illness, such as Post-Traumatic Stress Disorder (PTSD). This mental disorder may develop after a person is exposed to a traumatic experience, such as a horrific car accident, a sexual assaults or threats to a person's existence. On the battlefield veterans were exposed to much life threaten circumstances.

Despite being sought after by corporations, veterans continue to face challenges as they transition from the military. This is my contribution to my brother in Arms of bringing awareness to the stigmatization veterans' face in the civilian workplace.

Those who begin to plan for transition early are far better than those who wait. Hierarchy and following strict rules is what veterans are used to, but as they move from military to civilian organizations, veterans do face the problem of readjusting themselves to a new culture that is very much different from that of the military. Most feel their military service is respected by employers, but three in five veterans express concerns about cultural barriers. A new Rally Point Rasmussen Reports national survey of active and retired military personnel finds that thirty-eight percent consider the transition back to civilian life to be the most significant challenge facing veterans today. Twenty-four percent think finding civilian employment is the greatest challenge, while thirteen percent say that of health care. (Rasmussen, 2016)

Approximately, forty percent of veterans say most private companies do not view military experience as a professional asset, which is a main reason why some veterans fail to perform their duties with the skills they acquired during their service in the military.

It was found in a study that nearly two-thirds of veterans said they felt more purpose in the military than in their corporate jobs. Fifty six percent of female veterans said their corporate careers weren't meeting their goal of meaningful work, compared to forty-seven percent of male veterans.

While such numbers may not be encouraging, companies are starting to pay more attention to sort out issues raised in different reports, said Nicholas Armstrong, the Senior Director of Research and Policy at Syracuse University's *Institute for Veterans and Military Families*. That may be partly because just over half of veterans leave their first post-military job within a year. There is a shift from a focus on just hiring veterans to asking, "What are we doing to find better matches for their careers?

How to help the Veteran adjust to the workplace

A Corporate manager cannot automatically adjust in the military world; likewise, one cannot expect the veterans to do all the adapting. Therefore, managers and recruiters should step forward in covering the communication and language gap between veterans and the corporate world. In this regard, you can seek help from the experienced veterans since they are well aware of their mind set. Among hundreds of employees it's natural if a leader is unaware of a veteran's presence. So, a recommended solution to a supervisor or manager is to educate all the employees regarding the resources and how to utilize them. In this regard, make it a part of recruiting and orientation. Furthermore, employers can create a list and make it approachable even after hiring.

Discussion is the key to the solution; the veteran employee resource group will be a great idea. As their task is to initiate the conversation, make them feel part of the team, listen to their concerns and encourage them in the learning phase.

For the concluding note, besides implementing the above suggestions, companies are expected to bridge between the military and civilian culture. In this respect, veterans won't be a burden on the industry.

However, what you read is merely one side of the story, the problems veterans face, moving on to a civilian life are neglected. Undoubtedly corporations invest a large amount of money in recruiting them, but that does not finish up their obligations. The companies should understand that matching up with fellow civilians and learning new techniques and concepts demands patients and time. During the hiring of veterans, companies expect them to undergo a drastic shift since they are unaware of the corporate environment, their terminologies and business tactics, therefore, leading to neglect and lack of promotion opportunities in their career. CSM, USA (Ret.) Bart Womack, Veteran Strategy Officer at Randstad say that "veteran hiring is a mindset and a culture shift. The companies that excel at hiring veterans have mastered this shift from the top down." (Watson, Perry, Ripley, Chittum, 2017, p1).

For a veteran back from the war it's hard for them to adjust to civilian life. Therefore, leaders in workplaces should help them in making their first step in conforming to the new environment. Companies should establish a group to network veterans so that the unhappy ones can have someone to talk to and finding mentors for them (Taylor, 2009).

Veterans should be treated with great respect, especially the war veterans, as without them we would have never achieved so much. Assistance should be provided to them to help them adjust easily to civilian life.

Suggestions for organizations improving the situation

- Be aware of the variety of resources available to your employees.
- Make resources known and accessible to all employees.
- Encourage use of resources.
- Educate them
- Veteran Employee Resource Group (ERG)

Part Three

(All about Teams)

What Makes a Team Work or Fail?

As a new employee during your career working on a team or group is inevitable. In part three we will start from the very basic make up of teams.

Teams are not a new phenomenon according to the authors Robbins and Finley (2000) The New Why Teams Don't Work: What Goes Wrong and How to Make it Right. They have been in existence since prehistory, when someone came up with a problem that needed everyone's input and contributing members rejoiced in the outcome. In the early sixties, multifunctional teams existed in big business such as accounting, designing and all information services. The post-war era saw organizations concerned with customer service and increased profit where "a deep trench separated management from the world: management was the driving force behind the operation and the workers were the muscle." As time advanced, competition from foreign countries like Japan and Germany began eating away at the United States Markets. The old manufacturing plants came to a halt.

By the 1990s, the old hierarchy model was a thing of the past. Many organizations saw a team as a solution to solving issues dealing with strategic planning, especially in the areas of cost, productivity, training, customer service and now globalization. At present, teams are still evolving as technology changes and competition takes on different nuances.

A researcher cites, "as organizations downsize, merge and restructure in order to be more competitive, teams are much better than individuals to utilize a person's talents." Teams are flexible and they have the ability to quickly assemble and deploy without disruption to the organization. Teams are more productive with clear purposes and goals. They are more dedicated to completing the tasked assignment. Teams out-perform an individual any day and are much preferred by bigger organizations (Robbins, 2003)

There are many myths as well as facts about the capabilities of a team. One such myth is that teams are not always the answer. Putting people into groups doesn't ensure that the finished product will be a success. Because people have their own self-interests, personalities and moods, there are a number of uncertainties that arise. The unfortunate thing is the group process is inhibited short-term or indefinitely.

Managers blame the wrong causes for team failure. This is called misattribution error. This is caused by the managers who have a tendency to blame others for their poor leadership skills. Managers will blame every individual member of the team, resources or competing parties as a way to protect themselves or their egos.

So, why do teams fail? Researchers Katzenbach and Smith (1993), cites the reason is that people are fearful of increased responsibility brought on by the team. Teams are too time-consuming and there are uncertainties and risks in decision making. Other failures with teams are that some people are not coming together for their share of the work, which produces a strain on the team. This is called social loafing. If the team ignores this, then, according Dr. Yvonne Magee, author of Teams: Avoiding Pitfalls, this behavior takes a toll on the internal work relationship as well as productivity (Magee, 1997)

Because of the need for organizations to stay competitive, provide outstanding customer service and remain globally aware, organizations turn to teams. Team formation must be adapted to fit every situation because one type won't work for all instances. Therefore, there are different types of teams according to researcher Thompson, manager-led, self-managing, self-directing, and self-governing. In designing a team, its purpose must be clear at the beginning (Thompson, 2004)

How to Improve Your Teamwork & Your Team

At this point, many of the necessary skills and various approaches have been outlined to achieve true workplace cooperation, so we can now move on to a step-by-step approach to improving teamwork.

Writing a list of things that need to be done may be the most vital aspect of any preliminary routine. Without this, it is unlikely that you will productively reach your goal, while completing this step will result in improved time management.

- It is also important to begin delegating work in the early stages of preparation; even if it is just deciding what future projects will be delegated.

- This is also the point when scheduling should be determined, whether for meetings or project timelines.

After taking the time to complete these early stages of preparation, workplace cooperation is more likely to ensue. From there, it is important to analyze the outcomes, realizing whether what you are doing is having the impacts you were hoping to achieve.

Following these steps will allow you to maintain continued communication with others, which will allow for the natural, subconscious increase in teamwork.

Thinking strategically will ensure that these steps unfold with the best possible outcome. In order for everything to run smoothly and effectively, the team must work as a single unit to carry out these steps to completion.

In order for the team to work cohesively as a single unit, they must feel satisfied in their job; what helps an employee increase their productivity and creativity? It's called empowerment. The employee becomes satisfied in the workplace when they are empowered and given the opportunity to have ownership over their projects and careers. Empower your employees in order that your team might thrive. Consider this: when employers delegate authority and responsibility to their employees, this not only increases job enrichment and satisfaction along with decreasing job turnover within the organization, but it develops the individual employee and encourages him or her to stay with the organization. This assures that the organization maintains its competitive edge amongst their industry.

When reflecting on my own experience as a team leader, I emphasize to each member of my team that they must take ownership of their assigned work. In other words, they should be responsible for the tasks they are given. This ownership gives the team member a sense of empowerment, making their part in a project or task essential, while also encouraging them to achieve beyond expectations.

As a team leader, I follow five principles that empower my team members:

1. Trust in individuals – each member of the team has talents and abilities and, when joined together with other talented individuals, you have collective abilities and knowledge that can accomplish results in their own ways. Give them the autonomy to take charge of the situation or task. Have faith in your people.

2. Equip individuals with the necessary tools of success – give them the scope to connect with others within the company and outside the company such as vendors, customers and

potential future customers.

3. Acknowledge achievements – my organization has monthly gatherings for hails and farewells, but also to recognize the professional achievements of teams and individuals.

4. Decentralize decision making – as a team leader, my supervisor gives me latitude in charting the course for my team. As a team leader I also encourage my members to collaborate, not only with each other, but with other teams within the organization. This assures individual growth, encourages creativity, increases productivity and increases job satisfaction within the individual and the collective team.

5. Encourage collaboration – the workplace should be viewed as a collective and cooperative effort and not an environment of hard labor at the hands of the task master. Being isolated and forbidden to speak with others inhibits growth and creativity for individuals and the organization. Remember, one does not succeed alone.

Empowerment of individuals assures individual success and organizational success. This translates into the organization as a whole having a competitive advantage amongst its industry. This also enhances the workplace culture within the organization. Remember, whatever leadership role you play in the organization, if you allow people the opportunity to be creative and become responsible for themselves they will grow and make your job easier.

A Talk on Making Decisions within Teams

Decision-making: Pitfalls and Solutions of Teams

When you read in the newspaper and listen to the rhetoric about the corruption in corporations and those that are taking faltering steps towards bankruptcy, people losing their retirements and life savings, you have to wonder: where are all of the smart people whose job it is to advise the CEO of the deep, dark, dangerous waters? What decision was made in the boardrooms and conference rooms of those big corporations to get those companies back on track? Maybe there are no models to look at to see problems before they happen. Decision-making is an active component that teams must accomplish – no matter what team design, decision-making is key.

As mentioned previously, the success of the team depends on the skill level of its members. Low decision-making and problem-solving skills reflect on the outcome of productivity. On the other hand, teams can make a good decision but go about it the wrong way. The solution to that is to choose a decision-making approach. A good decision-making model is found in *Figure 1-1*.

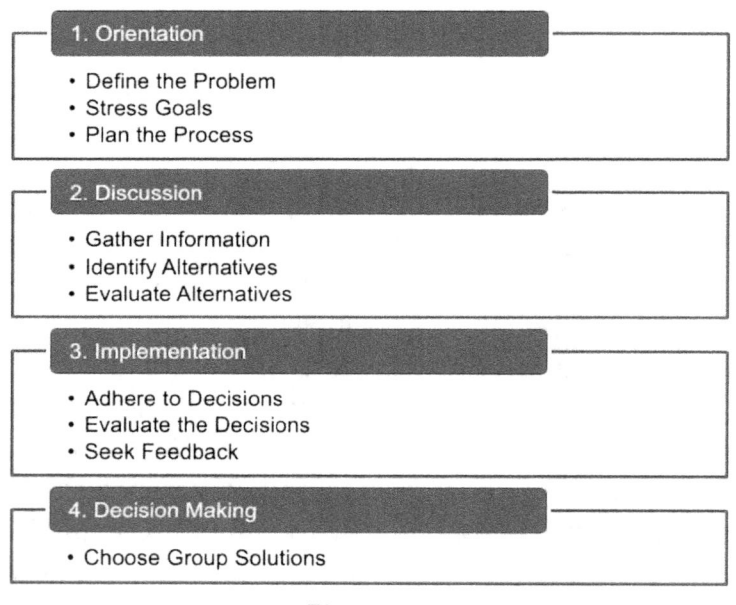

Figure 1-1

No matter what the type of problem (tactical problem-solving or creative), the steps should be followed in order to come out with a solid decision. Without this solid decision, the team will go down a path that will falter.

Individual versus Group Decision-Making

When is an individual decision better than a team decision? Most researchers agree team decisions are better because of the large pooling of resources that are available in order to solve problems . Diversity is the key in these areas. Levi gives three factors that must be in place in order for problem-solving to take place. First, a team must utilize their complementary core skills. This factor relates to the composition of the team . Remember, the people must have the ability to problem-solve, be knowledgeable in both technical and functional areas of their positions and they must have interpersonal skills. This makes the team decision superior to an individual decision (Levi, 2001)

Secondly, if good communication exists within the team, then everyone can discuss and pool their knowledge and ideas together. If poor communication exists, then the team's resources will not be utilized.

Thirdly, teams are better at solving complex problems because they are time consuming. Simple problems don't require the same lengthy thought processes; therefore, individuals would be the right choice.

Pitfalls to Decision-Making

There are two fundamental purposes/reasons for the existence of a team or group:

1. Decision-making
2. Performance

If one of these areas is inhibited then the team fails; everyone might as well just pack up and go home.

Now we will discuss two threats to decision-making that will affect the team, according to author Thompson (2004): group thinking and unethical decision-making .

Group-Think

Group-think is simply conformity to the team decision. It can be further defined as when norms of conformity to the group become stronger and members are more concerned about the unity of the group than critical evaluation of a problem. So, instead of a team member desiring to explore the problem and solution further, he or she stops the thought process and goes with the group decision in order to maintain the integrity of the group. There is a hesitancy to scrutinize dissimilar viewpoints within the group. There are well-known examples of group-think that costed American lives in politics and the corporate world. For instance, in 1941 Pearl Harbor, failure to protect Navy Fleet; in 1961 the Cuban missile crisis dubbed the "Bay of Pigs," the Vietnam War, the failed rescue attempt of the hostages at the US Embassy in Iran and the US Invasion of Iraq.

What are some of the symptoms of group-think? According to Thompson (2004), some of the symptoms are over-estimation of the group, which occurs when members exalt themselves above everyone else. Another symptom is close-mindedness, in which "members of the group engage in collective rationalization" often stereotyping other members of the group. Pressure towards uniformity is yet another symptom of group-think in which team members are forced to suppress their ideas and opinions for fear of social pressures from the group.

To avoid group-thinking, author Thompson first suggests a reduction in team size to no more than ten members. Secondly, invite different perspectives into the decision-making process. Thirdly, chose a person that is contradictory. A team needs a person that will challenge the status quo – a devil's advocate. Lastly, seek outside opinions in order to help the organization to form and shape the decision.

Unethical Decision-Making

So much is written on this type of threat to good decision-making because the bad decision starts from the top and slowly makes its way downward. According to Thompson (2004), 'unethical decision-making is an incremental descent into poor judgment.' When a company decides to entertain an unethical decision, they are counting on not being caught. Of course, there are always risks involved with not being caught, but what are they? People learn from each other: what I see you do and get away with, I may try, and expect the same results. If top management is practicing unethical things, then people will follow their unethical example. In the military, it's lead by example. According to author Thompson (2004), three conditions exist: Rational Man Model, Pluralistic Ignorance, and Desensitizing.

The author explains the Rational Man Model as one in which man tends to rationalize his own self-interest position. What is the motivating factor that maximizes his self-interest? As the old saying goes: "man tends to accommodate his own desire," so if you found money on a busy street, would you return it?

Pluralistic Ignorance

This threat to good decision-making is predicated on "I am not the only one undertaking this unethical behavior. If the boss is taking long lunch breaks then everyone else can do it." Not only is this condition laden with irresponsibility, it also shows a lack of concern for self-respect, or respect for others.

Desensitizing

This threat to good decision-making says that once an unethical decision is made, the second time is easier, and once it gets started it's hard to quit

To rid this behavior from your personal life or organization, author Thompson (2004) suggests three key methods; firstly, make everyone accountable for their behavior, secondly, reward good behavior in the company, and finally, eliminate conflicts of interest.

Diversity Differences

In today's competitive organization, variety is what counts. Diversity of ideas that are pooled and managed wisely can mean big dividends for the organization. People from different ethnic backgrounds bring different perspectives and viewpoints. The mixture can handle most of the complex problems in an organization. The demographics are changing and more minority men and women are now entering the workforce, and in large numbers - baby boomers are staying longer on the job. Relationships are changing between young and old, and there is a possibility that both will be working side by side.

From government to big business, everyone is harnessing the creative abilities of a diverse work force and using these generational ideas to achieve success.

Problems with Diversity

According to author Levi (2001), one of the main problems with diversity among team members is their misperception about other ethnic groups. People falsely stereotype a particular group of people and this reduces communication from minority team members, in addition to increasing emotional tension and conflict. In turn, the minority member communicates less, which is reflected in the decision-making. Diversity brings about an increase of information and different perspectives.

This valuable resource will be lost if the team ignores the views and opinions of the minority member. As my mother told my father, don't ignore the source of where the information is coming from.

Managing Diversity

How does an organization reduce the misconceptions and biases? The organization needs to design a program that increases awareness and knowledge of race and bias issues. Knowledge is power, and knowledge equals dollars.

One way to reduce these biases is to increase awareness through knowledge. Many organizations have programs that heighten awareness about different minority groups and misconceptions that surround them. But, on the other hand, this diversity training can heighten emotional tension, because of the uneasiness people get when attending these training sessions. This can lead to "polarization of attitudes about minorities, blaming and personal attacks," says author Levi (2001). So, awareness training needs to go beyond teaching about differences.

Improving Communication Skills

The basis of many conflicts within diverse groups is miscommunication, which is caused by stereotyping and distrust. The best way to deal with this problem is through communication. Team members can be trained to communicate better with other minorities and each other. Many organizations have skill-based programs in order to help members improve their communication skills to better manage diversity issues. When problems come up within the team, leaders should focus on the task and procedures outlined by the organization.

In essence, organizations can help teams better manage problems with diversity by developing programs to increase awareness of the different minority groups and improve the group ability to communicate better and resolve conflict when encountering diversity issues.

Team Leadership

Everyone knows that leadership is important to an organization, from corporations to the military. However, when it comes to leadership and teamwork, many have problems believing in its importance. The truth is that without leadership, teams don't experience their potential. Team leaders are the driving force behind an organization's success. To be an effective leader you must be able to coach the team, select your team players, develop the ability to have members work and coordinate and collaborate on the same level. According to author Thompson (2004), many organizations expect managers to take on the stellar role of becoming the team leader and do all of the mentoring and coaching. The problem is, Thompson continues, many managers don't know how to transform into these roles. Maybe this is because of resistance or change, but, on the other hand, leaders want more involvement but everyone is too afraid or they don't want the attention and pressures from their peers and mid-management.

The moment you implement these strategies for organizational communication, it creates a cycle of continuous improvement. Attributes such as resourcefulness and cooperation will only continue to develop.

Team Problem-Solving Skills

A team must be able to take on problems and challenges and evaluate what is available by way of solving the problem. Being able to diagnose problems and come up with solutions to them helps to build confidence in a team.

A team must have technical and functional skills in order to be successful. There are many interpretations of what types of skills are needed for a team or group to be effective in today's organizations. Most people agree that competence must be demonstrated among team members in knowing the inner workings of things. For example, if I hear a noise in my car, I wouldn't take the car to a medical doctor, no, I would take it to an auto mechanic, because they know the inner workings of the car. The mechanic is an expert. In medical terminology, he knows the anatomy and physiology. Moreover, a team member should know how to approach problems, especially in his or her area of expertise.

Interpersonal Skills

All team members should have the ability to communicate and know how to interact with individuals on a small and a large scale. In today's business world, the ability to work with cross-cultural groups is a great asset especially in a diverse society. Everyone looks at problems differently, and, as mentioned previously, people have different approaches to solving problems. Having individual people with high interpersonal skills can help to mitigate later conflicts and confrontations among team members.

Group Processes

Having the right people that are matched with the right tasks doesn't always guarantee success when tackling problems. Rosen (1989) agrees that having individuals coming together with different agendas, personalities and ethnic backgrounds, means that friction, rivalry, and competition will occur as individuals strive for dominance and security within a group. The good news is there is a high energy level being produced; the bad news is that the group process is interrupted along with motivation and true creativity. Groups/teams that don't reach their full potential have problems that are internal, which makes the group process unsuccessful. The author agrees that groups primarily engage in two types of activities: making decisions and performing tasks. (Levi, 2001).

The problem many teams have when faced with a task is that teams don't use the knowledge, skills and abilities available when engaged in the decision-making process. There are a number of reasons, as mentioned before, that groups encounter problems, some of which include: self-interest of the individuals, personal biases, or prejudice of the individuals. Another problem is that teams don't have clear goals or objectives outlined before the group process begins. Many experts agree that this is the reason why teams don't perform well during this process. According to author (Levi, 2001) highly effective teams are goal or task-oriented. Lack of performance in a team can bring or introduce negative behavior into the group where the productivity is affected among team members, commonly referred to as *social loafing.* Social loafing affects the performance of the team and the social loafer avoids being accountable to the purpose and goals of the group; therefore, group members must work harder in order to maintain a high, effective performance level.

Essentials of a successful Team

So, what is the bottom line of a successful team? What makes a team perform in order to reach its peak and perform well under pressure? Many researchers have a variety of perspectives of what is the make-up of successful teams a team and its members must have knowledge and skills; team must have motivation, both intrinsically and extrinsically and a team must have coordination and synchronicity amongst all members, just as a rowing team. Unless members are synchronized, they cannot experience success.

Organizational Context

The old saying goes: behind every successful man is a good woman (or vice versa). So, also, behind every successful team there should be an organization that cares and stands with their team, with resources necessary for the team's critical survival. A team needs the basic organizational structure that exists already in organizations such as tools, equipment and even a reward system. Without those raw materials, team performance is greatly inhibited. Furthermore, a supportive, organizational culture encourages open communication and cooperation between the team and its organization.

Types of Teams in Organizations

Manager-led teams

These teams are traditional where the manager or leader is responsible for monitoring progress and performance. Control dominates this group. An example of this is a military team (Special Forces) or a sports team.

Self-managing teams

A leader or manager who determines the overall purpose or goals of the team heads this team. This style is popular among organizations. Most self-managing teams are managerial task teams, according to author Thompson (2004); this team improves productivity, quality assurance and savings to the organization while at the same time promoting employee morale. It also reduces absenteeism and turnover, which can be factors as to why teams fail. An example of this is the steel industry. The use of self-managed teams helps to start new operations in order to stay competitive.

Self-directing teams

Before an organization designs a team that is almost autonomous, it should think twice before having control over the objectives and methods of achieving them. Self-directing teams can be extremely time-consuming and have the increased potential for conflict and can also be expensive to maintain. Self-directing teams have complete control over productivity, work responsibility, finances and scheduling of vacations and tasking. Another downfall can come in the form of different goals established by the team, which may not mirror that of the organization's. Self-directing teams are more suited for complex, ill-defined, or ambiguous problems.

Self-governing teams

This type of team is completely independent, usually utilizing a self-governing board of executives who are responsible for their own performance process designing the group. The problem with this type of team is that there is greater risk of misdirection. Individual team members could be at odds with upper management, therefore not going along with the organization's strategic goals. An example of this is an independent counsel.

Characteristics of a Successful Team

A successful team should be in harmony with each other. For example, a rowing team where everyone is rowing together with harmonious strides in rhythm, everyone pulling his or her weight and one at the stern to guide them. A diversified group approaches a task from distinctive points of view.

So, what is the object of a successful team? I feel that the object is to make the most of each team member's unique perspective. Again, to accomplish this goal, team players (members) must learn to identify not only their own style but also the styles of other teams and everyone must benefit. A team not only gets the job done by completing the task assigned, but skill level increases and broadens their perspective of other areas and management level of the organization. In my experience from being on a team, each new thing I learned about the company made me a little more marketable. People who don't experience this aura should not be on a team, because each member must be a contributor, a communicator, a collaborator, or a challenger.

Again, the more diverse a group is, the better the results of the final product.

Conditions for Successful Teams

According to (Levi, 2001), teams must have the right group of people to do the task. Secondly, the task must match the team. Thirdly, the teams must bring together their skills and ability in order to complete the task. Fourthly, the organization must support the team effort. People are what make success happen on a team and that success depends on the quality of skills people on the team have. Skills, most importantly, should correlate with the task.

In their book, *The Wisdom of Teams,* both authors outline the necessary skills needed in a team. They state that "the best way to understand a team is to look at the team itself ." This book highlights the team basis in a chart of performance results.

In order for the team to produce results, according to the authors, a team must have problem-solving skills, technical, functional and interpersonal skills along with accountability and commitment (Katzenbach & Smith, 1993).

Results & Outcomes of Cooperation

Cooperating in the workplace will allow you to secure a great deal of results, which will only continue to become more beneficial as time passes. Common outcomes include improved time management, the elimination of stress, increased trust among coworkers, improved scheduling and organizational skills and open communication.

Other outcomes may be found also, such as becoming a better team player.

Workplace cooperation takes a lot of effort. Thankfully, if you use the encouragement and guidelines offered in this book here while you work as a team at work, then you will be more than qualified for the task at hand.

As the author of this book said, at the beginning of this book "this edition is power pack." My wish is that the reader has learned something. If you are negating your way up the corporate ladder or a new employee remember navigating your way through your workplace. Remember, cooperating in the workplace demands action instead of passivity in which new employees will maintain the status quo. Furthermore, you can determine your own destiny as you put this book to practical use.

Congratulation on completing the 2nd edition of this book. cooperating in the workplace. Now you are on a more comprehensive and a confident journey through your organizational cultural, social and ethical wilderness as you are

Visit my blogsite: http://dcdardentalks.com

References

Abrams, M & Kennedy, J.T(2015). Mission Critical: Unlocking the value of Veterans in the Workforce. Retrieved from https://www.talentinnovation.com

Allport, G. W & Postman, L. (1947). *Psychology of rumor*. New York: Holt, Rinehart & Winston.
Anon. (2016). How millennials want to work and live. *Gallup*. Retrieved from https://www.gallup.com/workplace/238073/millennials-work-live.aspx

Armand, D. (2000). Bibliography on links among stress, violence, drug abuse, alcohol, tobacco in the workplace. Retrieved from http://www.oshanswers.ca/hscanada/stress_biblio.pdf

Army Leadership (1999). *Be, know, do*. Washington, D.C: Headquarters, Dept. of the Army,

Baer, H.P., Hess, M., 2008. Dangerous behavior in companies – individuals at risk and high-risk behavior. *In: Breitstadt, R., Kauert, G. (Eds.), The Worker – Risk Factor and Reliability*. Aachen: Shaker Verlag, 57–65.

Bahney, A., (2017). What millennials really want at work. *CNN Money*. Retrieved from https://money.cnn.com/2017/12/29/pf/millennials-work/index.html

Baker, C. (2007). "Sexual Harassment" Encyclopedia of Women in World History. Retrieved from https://scholarworks.smith.edu/cgi/viewcontent.cgi?

Baker, C. N. (2007). The emergence of organized feminist resistance to sexual harassment in the United States in the 1970s. *Journal of Women's History, 19*(3), 161-184.

Bowling, T. A., & Beehr (2006). Workplace harassment from the victim's perspective: a theoretical model and meta-analysis. *The Journal of Applied Psychology 91*(5), 988-1012.

Brack, J, and Kelly, K. (2012) Maximizing millennials in the workplace. *Kenan-Flagler Business School*. Retrieved from www.kenan-flagler.unc.edu/executive-development/custom-programs/~/media/files/documents/executive-development/maximizing-millennials-in- the-workplace.

Buzz Marketing Group and the Young Entrepreneur Council (2011). Youth entrepreneurship survey. Retrieved from https://www.slideshare.net/twfashion/yecbuzz-marketing-group-youth-entrepreneurship-study

Califf, R. M., Woodcock, J., & Ostroff, S. (2016). A proactive response to prescription opioid abuse. *New England Journal of Medicine, 374*(15), 1480-1485.

Cauldron, S. (1998). On the contrary: they heard it through the grapevine. *Workforce, 77*(11), 25-27.

Chipman, M., and Jin, Y.L. (2009). Drowsy drivers: the effect of light and circadian rhythm on crash occurrence. *Safe Science, 47*(10), 1364–1370.

Crenshaw, D (2008). *The myth of multitasking: how doing it all gets nothing done*. San Francisco: Jossey-Bass.

Darden, D. (2017). *Cooperating in the workplace*. California: CreateSpace Independent Publishing Platform.

Degenhardt, L. and Hall, W. (2012). Extent of illicit drug use and dependence, and their contribution to the global burden of disease. *Lancet, 379*, 55–70.

Delbridge, R. & Noon, M. (1993). News from behind my hand: gossip in organizations. *Organization Studies, 14*(1), 23-26.

Djurkovic, N., McCormack, D. & Casimir, G. (2004). The physical and psychological effects of workplace bullying and their relationship to intention to leave: a test of the psychosomatic and disability hypotheses.

International Journal of Organization Theory and Behavior, 4, 469-497.

Dukes, E., (2017, March 7). 3 things your workplace does that millennials hate. *Inc.* Retrieved from https://www.inc.com/elizabeth-dukes/3-things-your-workplace-does-that-millennials-hate.html

Dumas, C. & Sankowsky, D (1998). Understanding the charismatic leader-follower relationship: promises and perils. *Journal of Leadership Studies, 5*(4), 29.

Emily, G. (2015, January 02). How does drug abuse affect society and you? Retrieved from http://www.drugrehab.org/how-does-drug-abuse-affect-society-and-you/

Federal Government (2012). *One in eight feds have witnessed workplace violence in past two years.* Baltimore, MD: Federal Government Publication.

Feess, E., Mueller, H. and Ruhnau, S. G. (2014) The impact of religion and the degree of religiosity on work ethic: a multilevel analysis. *International Review for Social Sciences, 67*(4), 506-534.

Forsyth, D. (1990). *Anatomy of group decision making.* 2nd ed. Pacific Grove, CA: Brooks, Cole.

Frost, S. (2018). How to cooperate as a team member in a workplace. *Small Business –*

Chron.com. Retrieved from
http://smallbusiness.chron.com/cooperate-team-member-workplace-11347.html

Fry, R. (2018, March 1). Millennials projected to overtake baby boomers as America's largest generation. *Pew Research Center.* Retrieved from http://www.pewresearch.org/fact-tank/2018/03/01/millennials-overtake-baby-boomers/

Gallup (2016, May 11). What millennials want from work and life. *Gallup.com.* Retrieved from news.gallup.com/businessjournal/191435/millennials-work-life.aspx

Gerdes, L. I. (1999). *Sexual harassment.* San Diego, CA:Greenhaven Press., 87-89

Gilani, N. (2017, September 26). Importance of cooperation in the workplace. *Bizfluent.* Retrieved from https://bizfluent.com/info-8680017-importance-cooperation-workplace.html

Greer, L. L. (2014). Power in teams: Effects of team power structures on team conflict and team outcomes. *Stanford.* Retrieved from https://www.gsb.stanford.edu/faculty-research/publications/power-teams-effects-team-power-structures-team-conflict-team-outcomes

Haltiwanger, J., Jarmin, R., and Miranda, J. (2012) Business dynamics statistics briefing: where have all the young firms gone? *Kauffman.* Retrieved from https://www.census.gov/ces/pdf/BDS_StatBrief6_Yo ung_Firms.pdf

Hannam, S. & Yordi, B. (2011). Engaging a multi-generational workforce: practical advice for government managers. *IBM Center for the Business of Government*. Retrieved from http://www.businessofgovernment.org/report/engagi ng-multi-generational-workforce-practical-advice-government-managers.

Hardy, M. M. & Upshaw. D. (2016). What do millennials want in the perfect workplace environment? Retrieved from http://ijier.net/ijier/article/view/3/2
Harris Interactive (2010) Youth pulse 2010

Kauffman foundation custom report. *Kauffman*. Retrieved from http://www.kauffman.org/uploadedFiles/youth_eship _report_2010.

Hersch, J. (2015). Sexual harassment in the workplace. *IZA World of Labor 2015,* 188. doi: 10.15185/izawol.188

Hogh, A., Hoel, H. and Caneiro, I. G. (2011). Bullying and employee turnover among health-care workers; a three-wave prospective study. *Journal of Nursing Management 19*(6),742-51.

Hunt, C., Davidson, M., Fielden, S., & Hoel, H. (2007). Sexual harassment in the workplace: A literature review. *Equal Opportunities Commission Working Paper Series, 59.*

Irvine., R. (1995). Workplace violence, what to do when tragedy strikes. *APR Study Guide, Public Relations Tactics.*

Jones, C., (2018). More Millennials want freelance careers instead of working full-time. *USA Today.* Retrieved from https://www.usatoday.com/story/money/2018/04/15/millennials-more-interested-freelance-careers/512851002/

Joubert, P., Van Wyk, C. & Rothmann, S. (2011). The effectiveness of sexual harassment policies and procedures at higher education institutions in South Africa. *SA Journal of Human Resource Management, 9*(1), 1-10.

Juliano, A. C. (2007). Harassing women with power: The case for including contra-power harassment within Title VII. *Bul Rev., 87,* 491.

Katzenbach, J. R. & Smith, K. (1993). *The wisdom of teams: creating the high-performance.* NY: Harvard Business School Press.

Kauert, G. & Breitstadt, R. (2008). The effects of illicit drugs – a comparison of the potential for influence. *In: The Worker – Risk Factor and Reliability.* Aachen: Shaker Verlag, 23–27.

Kimmel, A. (2004). *Rumors and rumor control: a manager's guide to understanding and combating rumors*. Mahwah, NJ: Lawrence Erlbaum Assoc. Kozlowski, S. W. J., & Ilgen, D. R. (2006). Enhancing the effectiveness of work groups and teams. *Psychological Science in the Public Interest, Supplement, 7*(3), 77-124. DOI: 10.1111/j.1529-1006.2006.00030.x.

Lee, W. A. (2015, June). Health and behavioral risks of alcohol and drug use. Retrieved from https://www.wlu.edu/student-life/health-and-safety/student-health-and-counseling/health-library/alcohol-and-other-drugs/health-and-behavioral-risks-of-alcohol-and-drug-use.

Lepak, D. & Gowan, M. (2016). *Human resources management: managing employees for competitive advantage*. 2nd ed. Chicago: Chicago Business Press.

Levi, D. (2001). *Group dynamics*. Thousand Oaks, CA: Sage Publications, Inc.

Li, Y. and Bai., Y (2008) Comparison of characteristics between fatal and injury accidents in the highway construction zones. *Safe Science, 46*(4), 646-660.

Lipka, M. (2015) Millennials increasingly are driving growth of 'nones'. *Pew Research Center*. Retrieved from www.pewresearch.org/fact-tank/2015/05/12/millennials-increasingly-aredrivinggrowth-of-nones.

Locke, E. A., & Schattke, K. (2018). Intrinsic and extrinsic motivation: Time for expansion and clarification. *Motivation Science*. doi:10.1037/mot0000116

Lopes, H., Santos, A., & Teles, N. (2009). The motives for cooperation in work organizations. *Journal of Institutional Economics, 5*(3), 315-338. doi:10.1017/S1744137409990038

Loukopoulos, D., Dismukes, K. and Barshi, I. (2008). *The multitasking myth*. Farnham: Ashgate Publishing.

Magee, Y. S. (1997). S teams: avoiding the pitfalls. *Public Management*, 79(7), 26+.

May, G. L. (2003). Group dynamics for teams. *The Journal of Business Communication, 40*(3), 241+.

McCready, R. (2016, June 7). Millennials don't suck, you're just old and hate change. *Insider.* Retrieved from https://thenextweb.com/insider/2016/06/07/millennials-dont-suck-youre-just-old-hate-change/

McGregor, J. (2015, November 11). The problems veterans face in the professional workplace. *Washington Post.* Retrieved from https://www.washingtonpost.com/news/on-leadership/wp/2015/11/11/the-problems-veterans-face-in-the-professional-workplace.

McLaughlin, H., Uggen, C. & Blackstone, A. (2012). Sexual harassment, workplace authority, and the paradox of power. *American Sociological Review, 77*(4), 625-647.

McLaughlin, H., Uggen, C., & Blackstone, A. (2017). The economic and career effects of sexual harassment on working women. *Gender & Society, 31*(3), 333-358.

Melton, J. (2003). When teams work best. *Business Communication Quarterly, 66*(3), 133+.

Merkin, R. S. (2012). Sexual harassment indicators: the socio-cultural and cultural impact of marital status, age, education, race, and sex in Latin America. *Intercultural Communication Studies, 21*(1).

Myers, K. and Sadaghiani, K. (2010). Millennials in the workplace: a communication perspective on millennials' organizational relationships and performance. *Journal of Business and Psychology, 25*(2): 225–238.

Myers, K., & Sadaghiani, K. (2010). Millennials in the workplace: a communication perspective on millennials' organizational relationships and performance. *Journal of Business and Psychology, 25*(2), 225-238.

Northouse, P. G. (2004). *Leadership: theory and practice.* Thousand Oaks, CA: Sage Publications Ltd.

Northwestern National Life Insurance Company (U.S.) Employee Benefits Division. (1993). *Fear and violence in the workplace: a survey documenting the experience of American workers.* Northwestern National Life.

Outwardbound. (2017, February 21). Scientific Study details the impact of outward bound for veterans [Blog post]. Retrieved from https://www.outwardbound.org/blog/scientific-study-details-impact-outward-bound-veterans/

Pew Research Center (2013, December 11). Chapter 4: men and women at work. *Pew Research Center.* Retrieved from http://www.pewsocialtrends.org/2013/12/11/chapter-4-men-and-women-at-work/

Ramsaroop, A., & Parumasur, S. B. (2007). The prevalence and nature of sexual harassment in the workplace: A model for early identification and effective management thereof. *SA Journal of Industrial Psychology, 33*(2), 25-33.

Rasmussen, W. J. (2016). Perceived barriers to reporting military sexual assault: an interpretative phenomenological analysis. *PhD (Doctor of Philosophy) thesis, University of Iowa.*

Retrieved from
https://ir.uiowa.edu/cgi/viewcontent.cgi?article=6821
&context=etd

Robbins, H. & Finley, M. (2000). *The new why teams don't work: what goes wrong and how to make it right.* 2nd ed. California: Berrett-Koehler Publishers.

Robbins, S. (2004). *Essentials of organizational behavior.* 8th ed. New Jersey: Pearson Prentice Hall.

Robbins, S. P. (2003). *Organizational behavior.* 11th ed. Upper Saddle River, NJ: Prentice Hall.

Roehling, M. V., & Huang, J. (2018). Sexual harassment training effectiveness: An interdisciplinary review and call for research. *Journal of Organizational Behavior, 39*(2), 134-150.

Rosen, C. (2008). The myth of multitasking. *The New Atlantis*, 105-110.

Rosen, N. (1989). *Teamwork and the bottom line groups make a difference.* Hillsdale: Lawrence Erlbaum Associates.

Schat, A. C. H., Frone, M. R., & Kelloway, E. K. (2006). Prevalence of Workplace Aggression in the U.S. Workforce: Findings from a National Study. *In E. K. Kelloway, J. Barling, & J. J. Hurrell (Eds.), Handbook of Workplace Violence (pp. 47-89).*

Thousand Oaks, CA: Sage.
https://doi.org/10.4135/9781412976947.n4

Schreiner, E. (2018). Importance of cooperation in the workplace. Retrieved from https://woman.thenest.com/importance-cooperation-workplace-14647.html

Schuckjt M. A. (2009). Alcohol-use disorders. *The Lancet, 373,* 492-501.

Siegel, R. B. (2003). Introduction: a short history of sexual harassment. *In Directions in sexual harassment law.* Yale University Press.

Silver, S. (2000). *Organized to be your best.* USA: Adams-Hall Publishing.

Softchalk. (2016). Impact of substance abuse. Retrieved from https://www.softchalk.com/lessonchallenge10/lesson/corp%20

Stander, V. A., & Thomsen, C. J. (2016). Sexual harassment and assault in the US military: A review of policy and research trends. *Military medicine, 181*(suppl_1), 20-27.

Stojanovic, M. (2015). Get serious about a healthy workplace. *Drugs and alcohol,* 7-8.
Strauss, K. (2016). How veterans adjust to the civilian workforce. *Forbes.* Retrieved from

https://www.forbes.com/sites/karstenstrauss/2016/1
1/11/how-veterans-adjust-to-the-civilian-
workforce/#52ab6aa26711

Sutton, C. L. & Konzelmann, S. J. (1998). Self-
managed teams in the steel industry: an interview
with John Selky. *Journal of Leadership Studies,*
7(2), 96.

Taylor, S. (2009, November 4). Companies help
veterans adapt to civilian workplace. Retrieved from
https://www.shrm.org/resourcesandtools/hr-
topics/employee-
relations/pages/companieshelpveterans.aspx

The Economic Times (2017, July 14). Challenges
faced by millennials at the workplace. Retrieved
from
https://economictimes.indiatimes.com/jobs/challeng
es-faced-by-millennials-at-the-
workplace/challenges-faced-by-millenials-at-the-
workplace/slideshow/59598004.cms

Thompson, L. L. (2004). *Making the team: a guide
for managers.* Westford, MA: Pearson Education
LTD. 8, 10,13,17,23,46,53,55.

Trent R. B. (1991). Emergency room evidence on
the role of alcohol intoxication in injury at work in the
US. *Saf. Sci., 14*(3–4), 241-252.

U.S. Chamber of Commerce Foundation (2012,
November). The Millennial Generation, Nation

Chamber Foundation. Retrieved from https://www.uschamberfoundation.org/reports/millennial-generation-research-review

U.S. Small Business Administration (2012) FY 2012 Congressional Budget Justification. Retrieved from http://www.sba.gov/sites/default/files/FINAL%20FY%202012%20CBJ%20FY%202010%20APR_0.

Varanelli, A. (2009, December 09). Some thoughts for veterans and disabled veterans on employment issues [Blog post]. Retrieved from http://www.pbs.org/pov/regardingwar/conversations/coming-home/some-thoughts-for-veterans-and-disabled-veterans-on-employment-issues.php

Volkow, N. D., & McLellan, A. T. (2016). Opioid abuse in chronic pain—misconceptions and mitigation strategies. *New England Journal of Medicine, 374*(13), 1253-1263.

Watson, K .W., Perry, M., Ripley,B., Chittum, R.(2017). Retrieved from https://hbr.org/2017/07/how-your-company-can-better-retain-employees-who-are-veterans

Weaver, J. (2012). Diversity can benefit teamwork in a STEM. *Center for Teaching & Learning*. Retrieved from teaching.berkeley.edu/diversity-can-benefit-teamwork-stem.

William, H. (2017). Diversity defines the millennial generation. *Brookings*. Retrieved from www.brookings.edu/blog/the-avenue/2016/06/28/diversity-defines-the-millennial-generation/.

Wilmer, H., Sherman, E. L. and Chein, J. M. (2017). Smartphones and cognition: a review of research exploring the links between mobile technology habits and cognitive functioning. *Front Psychol.*, *8*, 605.

Young Invincibiles (2011). Young invincibles policy brief. *Kauffman.* Retrieved from https://www.kauffman.org/-/media/kauffman_org/research-reports-and-covers/2011/11/millennials_study.pdf

Zapf, D., Einarsen, S., Hoel, H. & Vartia, M. (2003). Empirical findings on bulling in the workplace: on bulling and emotional abuse in the workplace. *In Bullying and Emotional Abuse in the Workplace, 44*, 103-126.

Visit the following websites for more information:

www.drugabuse.gov
www.NIH.gov
www.HHS.gov

Kittie W. Watson Michael Perry Becky Ripley Randy Chittum